DYSLEXIA EXPLAINED

Without the need for too many words...

Written by Mike Jones & Illustrated by Leah Heming

WHO IS NESSY ?

Nessy has been making fun and multisensory educational software that supports learners with dyslexia and learning disabilities since 1999.

Since its launch Nessy has built a reputation for exceptional quality. For three successive years Nessy has won the prestigious Educational Resources Award for Special Educational Needs.

Nessy programs are used in schools worldwide to help children rebuild self-confidence, rediscover self-esteem and establish a love of learning. Independent research studies on Nessy Reading and Spelling show that students who use the program can increase their reading abilities by up to 2 years in as little as 18 weeks!

THE AUTHOR'S STORY

Mike Jones is a parent, entrepreneur and has dyslexia. At 9 years old Mike could not read or even spell his own name. To help, his mother homeschooled him for a year and created a series of techniques that greatly developed his ability to understand and retain information. His mother's intervention transformed Mike's ability to retain information and he soon went from bottom of the class straight to the top.

When Mike left school, he went on to study law whilst his mother set up a school to help other children with dyslexia. In his free time, Mike helped out by answering the telephone at her school. Mike recalls how conversations all started the same way with parents desperate for help.
Mike knew that he needed to take the successful techniques that had helped him and make them available online for everyone. In 1999, Mike launched Nessy Learning: a company that aims to support learners with dyslexia and learning disabilities. To date, more than 20,000 schools and hundreds of thousands of children have used his programs worldwide.

PRAISE FOR NESSY LEARNING

"At the age of 8 I found out that I had dyslexia. This really worried me as I thought people would treat me differently and I wouldn't fit in. Nessy helped me to overcome this fear as it gave me a lot of confidence with reading and spelling."

Lucy

"The first time I met Nessy he was in the computer but now he is in my head and when my class are doing a big write Nessy is helping me. I just open the door in my head and Nessy is there to help."

Eve

"Dear Nessy, when I moved school I had to catch up two years of learning to read and write. I felt very nervous starting Nessy. I didn't know the alphabet but all the other children already knew how to read and write. It has been two years and now I know how to read and write and caught up with all the other children. Thank you Nessy for helping me to read and write."

Nina

"If you are looking for a hilarious game that will also improve your reading skills then you should try Nessy! Our class uses Nessy every Wednesday. Last week we had a spelling test on words with silent consonants. Luckily I had just reviewed the lesson on silent consonants the week before on Nessy. I got 100% on my test! I love playing the games, especially because they help me learn."

Graciela

These comments have been received from children using Nessy.

"My son, who is 9 years old and has dyslexia, has been using the Nessy program. He has greatly improved and now enjoys reading."

Sharon

"I adore using this program as it inspires the children I teach. The phonic sounds and animated rules are excellent for helping children with their memory."

Joan

"Just wanted to say a massive **THANK YOU** for really helping our severely dyslexic son."

Tabbie

"It teaches the students without them realizing that they are being taught because they are having so much fun."

Janet

These comments have been received from parents & teachers.

INTRODUCTION

This book helps parents understand dyslexia:
the positives, the difficulties and what helps.
After reading, use it to help explain dyslexia to your child.
Sections suitable for children show this icon:

GOOD FOR SHARING

Dyslexia causes low self-esteem. It makes learning to read and
write much harder and affects the whole family. Every person
with dyslexia needs to find the mental strength to
get through school.
The first step on that journey is to understand dyslexia
and rediscover the self-belief and determination to succeed.
People with dyslexia tend to think in pictures rather than words
so illustrations are used to explain each point.
We hope you enjoy this book.

CHAPTER 1

understanding dyslexia

Dyslexia was discovered more than 100 years ago.

But many people still don't understand it.

discovered by Doctor Berlin in **1887**

Dyslexia is passed through families.

dyslexic

dyslexic

grandad grandma grampy granny cousin

uncle mum dad uncle

me ← dyslexic

Do you know someone in your family with dyslexia?

1 in 5 people have dyslexia.

Dyslexia is neurological.
The dyslexic brain processes written
and spoken information differently.

Sometimes the information is forgotten,
jumbled up or bits are missing.

Problems when reading

Difficulties when writing

Tough tasks

Finishing
on time

Recalling
A c D
Q T
names

Staying
focused

Doesn't like school

unhappy 😞

angry and frustrated 😠

withdrawn and quiet 😐

SUMMARY

Dyslexia is a difference in the way the brain processes words.

However, it affects much more than reading and writing. It also causes difficulty with organization, math and memory.

CHAPTER 2
types of dyslexia

VISUAL PROCESSING DYSLEXIA

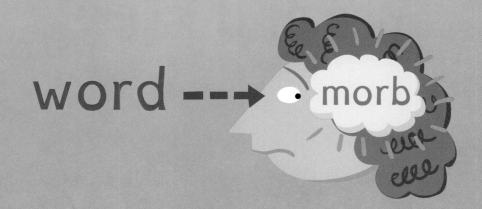

Visual difficulties

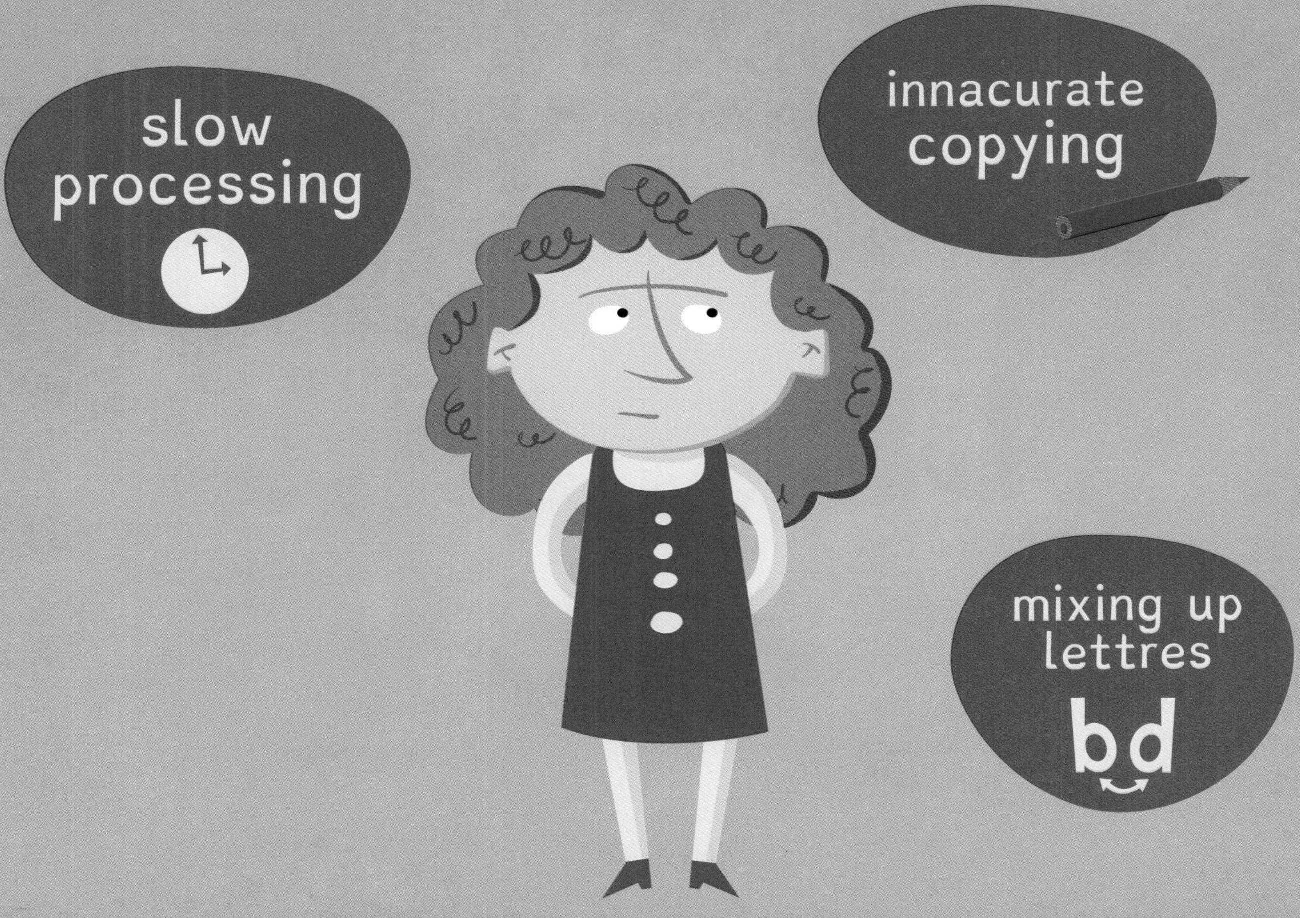

AUDITORY
(hearing)
PROCESSING
DYSLEXIA

word ---> wrod

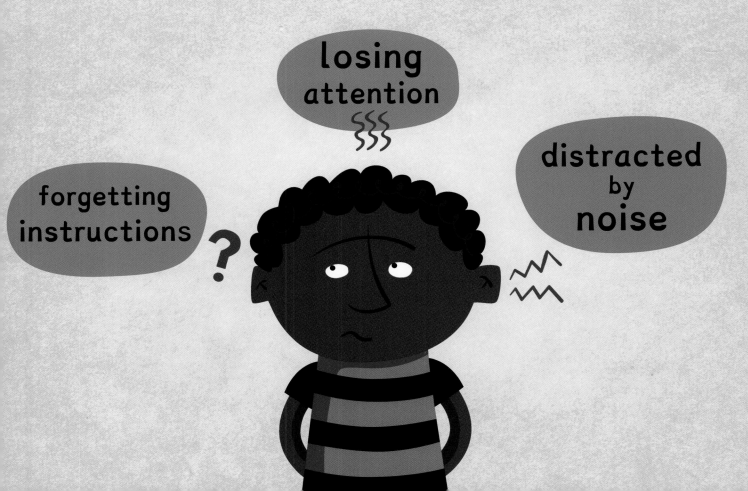

SLOW PROCESSING SPEED

SPEED

(it takes much Longer)

WORKING
MEMORY
DYSLEXIA

work in progress

Working memory can store between
5 and 7 chunks of information.

But those with dyslexia struggle to remember even 3.

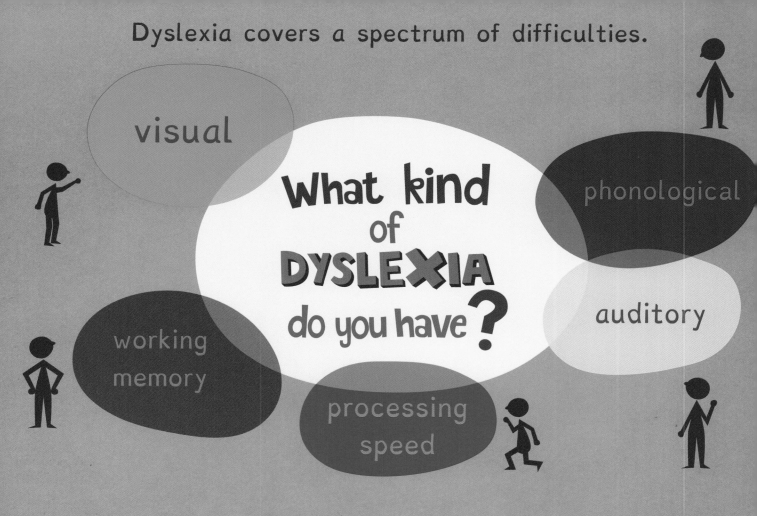

SUMMARY

Every person is slightly different depending upon what sort of dyslexia they have. It is important to find out what type of dyslexia you have. This will help you to find out which learning approach will work best.

Try Dyslexia Quest.

A 20 minute dyslexia screener.

CHAPTER 3
what dyslexic people are good at...

GOOD FOR SHARING

Seeing the bigger picture

People with dyslexia have the ability to imagine how everything works together and picture how things will end up. This is a great leadership skill.

Thinking outside the box

People with dyslexia are able to see things
from a different angle and come up with unusual ideas.

Being able to **imagine** a vision of the future combined with an **unconventional** approach has helped
some people with dyslexia become **successful entrepreneurs.**

Steve Jobs
creator of Apple

Spatial awareness

People with dyslexia are better at imagining
how objects and spaces will connect.

Some of the world's leading architects have dyslexia.

Spatial understanding helps them to develop their ideas into amazing buildings.

Richard Rogers
architect

Creative ideas

Benjamin Zephaniah
poet, writer
and musician

Even though dyslexia
causes difficulties
with the process
of reading and writing
it doesn't stop you
being very creative
with words.

Famous actors with dyslexia

Some people with dyslexia
channel this creativity into acting.

Whoopi Goldberg
actor

Keira Knightley
actor

Orlando Bloom
actor

Picture thinking

People with dyslexia are often visual thinkers and this makes them good at problem solving.

Pattern recognition

Top code breakers are able to crack complex problems because their dyslexia helps them find patterns.

Many talented scientists have dyslexia.

Christopher Tonkin
scientist

Astrophysicists with dyslexia are better
at detecting unusual details in large images of space.

SUMMARY

Creativity, strong visualization, problem solving abilities and an unconventional way of looking at things have helped many people with dyslexia to succeed in life.

Think about what you are good at and choose a path that uses your strengths.

CHAPTER 4
dyslexia
difficulties

Words get jumbled in my head.

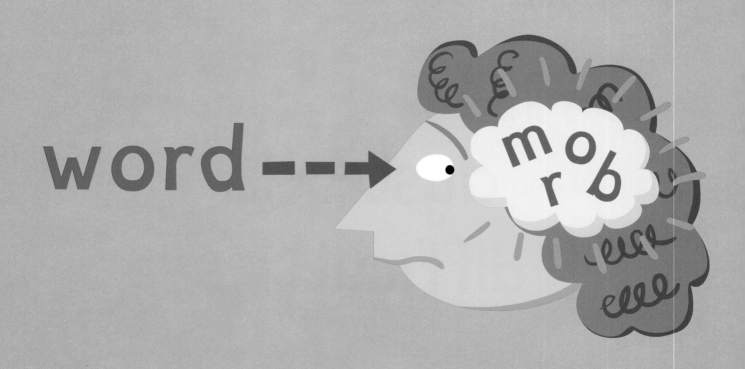

word --->

The word sounds right but looks wrong.

with   wiv

was   wos

they   thay

I often forget silent letters when I spell.

stick
white
friends
huge

stik
wite
frends
hug

Sometimes I reverse numbers and letters.

I have difficulty copying.

I am slower at writing.

Sometimes it seems like

my brain hops over words.

I make mistakes when I read out loud.

I have trouble recalling instructions.

I have difficulty remembering a sequence of steps.

Like tying a knot.

People with dyslexia often lose or forget things.

SUMMARY

Most children will show difficulties like this for a short while but will quickly develop their abilities.

For many children with dyslexia, the difficulties will be more severe and persistent, causing them to fall behind.
Every individual with dyslexia is different and no one will have all these difficulties.
It depends on what type of dyslexia you have.

CHAPTER 5
helpful strategies

Using mnemonic memory strategies
helps to spell difficult words.

Was
A
Sausage

Mispronouncing words can also help you spell.

busy

Learning syllables helps to read
and spell long words.

Linking sounds to a funny picture helps to split the syllables.

Linking a picture to a word will make it easier to learn.
To remember lots of words, link the pictures into a story.

MY CAT

school
Letter

gym kit

Library
books

Picture thinking can help you remember names.

MIKE   LORRAINE   FRED

SUMMARY

Looking at words and copying them is not an effective way for people with dyslexia to learn to spell but there are many learning strategies that can help.

CHAPTER 6

what works best for dyslexia?

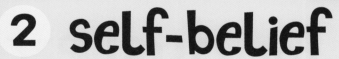

3 success

2 self-belief

1 reward small achievements

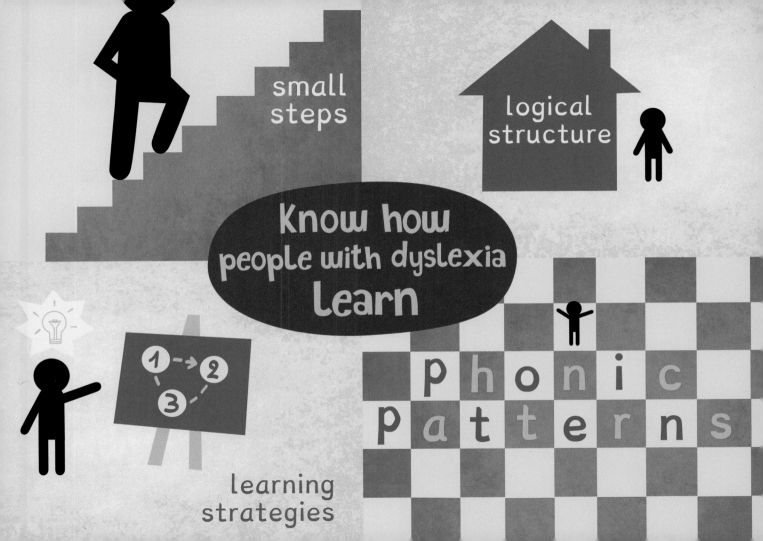

ai ph oi ue sh ea th

air  ie

oy ar

ear ee

ch au oo aw er ay wh

SEE IT

→ word

SAY IT

word

use
multisensory
learning

HEAR IT

◁ word

WRITE IT

word

1 Identify my difficulties.

2 Work at my pace.

use an individualized approach

3 Find helpful strategies.

4 Learn what I need.

CAT

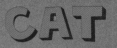

link pictures
to sounds
and words

spelling rules

magic **e**

understand the **structure** of **language**

rhyming
and blending

THINK

STINK

syllables, prefixes
and **suffixes**

po ta to

recognize that everyone has different strengths

What is your strength?

visual thinking

listening saying

actions

SUMMARY

Individuals with dyslexia benefit from a supportive environment combined with an individualized, multisensory program of learning, structured into small steps.

The **N**essy **R**eading and **S**pelling program has been designed to include all of these strategies for success.